THE POWER
WITHIN

Achieve True Greatness
Remove Self-imposed Limitations

THE POWER
WITHIN

Written by
Vikki Jones

VMH Publishing

The publisher is not responsible for the content within this
book, websites, or social media pages (or their content)
related to this publication, that are not owned by the
publisher. Quantity sales.

Special discounts are available on quantity purchases by
corporations, associations, and others.

Hardback ISBN: 979-8-9903203-2-1
Paperback ISBN: 979-8-9903203-0-7
E-Book: 979-8-9903203-1-4

Published in United States of America

10 9 8 7 6 5 4 3 2

VMH Publishing
New York, NY

Table of Contents

Introduction

"The Power Within" is a compelling and transformative journey that invites you to unlock the extraordinary potential that lies within each of us. In a world filled with uncertainties and obstacles, it's easy to overlook the immense power that resides within our own being. You might have heard the saying, "You have what it takes," but do you truly believe it? This book is here to remind you that no matter who you are, where you currently stand in life, or which career path you've chosen, the ability to live the life you desire exists within you.

It's true; achieving your dreams and living a fulfilling life may require hard work, innovation, and a dash of creativity. Yes, you might need to think outside the box, but here's the bottom line – it's entirely possible. The key is recognizing the potential you possess, learning how to tap into that power, develop it, and utilize it to not only enhance your own existence but also leave a positive impact on those around you.

This book is more than just a guide; it's a mirror that reflects your true essence, revealing the strength and capabilities that may be hidden within. Through practical tips, transformative mindset shifts, and the art of personal storytelling, "The Power Within" is dedicated to unveiling the greatness that resides inside of you.

You see, what many people fail to realize is that the answers they seek, the strength they long for, and the change they desire are already present within them. All too often, we search externally for what can only be discovered internally.

This journey is not about finding something new; it's about uncovering something that has always been there. Each chapter will provide you with the tools, insights, and revelations necessary to recognize and harness this incredible power.

So, if you're ready to embark on a compelling expedition of self-discovery, if you're eager to unveil the dormant strength and abilities lying within your core, then prepare yourself for an extraordinary odyssey.

Open your mind, open your heart, and let's set forth on this journey of empowerment and self-realization. Within the pages of this book, you will find the guidance you need to connect with your inner potential, unleashing the power within to shape a life of purpose, fulfillment, and boundless impact.

Get ready to embrace the greatness that lies within you. It's time to embark on a transformative voyage where the destination is not a far-off place, but rather a profound understanding and appreciation of the extraordinary being that you are.

Chapter 1

*The Essence of Personal Power -
Understanding the Fuel of Greatness*

Personal power is the inner strength that
helps people take control of their lives and
reach their goals. In our world filled with
endless possibilities and opportunities, there
exists a fundamental force that drives us to
achieve greatness - personal power. But
what exactly is personal power, and how can
one tap into its essence to unlock their full
potential?

Personal power can be defined as the inner
strength and confidence that enables us to
take control of their lives, make decisions,
and pursue their goals with conviction. It is
the driving force behind success, resilience,
and fulfillment in every aspect of life.

But personal power is not just about

physical strength or assertiveness. It goes beyond mere external measures of success and encompasses a deep sense of self-awareness, emotional intelligence, and the ability to harness your unique talents and abilities.

To truly understand the essence of personal power, one must first recognize that it is not something that can be obtained through external validation or material possessions. Instead, personal power stems from a deep sense of self-worth and belief in your capabilities.

Harnessing personal power requires a willingness to embrace vulnerability, face challenges head-on, and embrace failure as a stepping stone to growth. It is about being authentic, honest, and true to oneself, even in the face of adversity.

As you tap into their personal power, they begin to cultivate a sense of inner strength and resilience that allows them to navigate life's ups and downs with grace and confidence. They become the masters of their own destiny, able to channel their energy and focus towards achieving their dreams and aspirations.

In the journey towards personal power, it is important to remember that greatness is not defined by external measures of success or the approval of others. Instead, true greatness lies in the ability to cultivate a sense of inner strength, confidence, and authenticity that allows one to shine brightly in a world filled with endless possibilities.

As you move forward on your journey towards personal power, remember that the fuel of greatness lies within you. Remove any self-imposed limitations, embrace your uniqueness, cultivate your strengths, and believe in your ability to achieve anything you set your mind to. Because true personal power is not just about what you do, but who you are becoming in the process.

Here are a few suggestions that help to understand your personal power:

- Self-Reflection: Take time to explore your inner strengths, weaknesses, values, and beliefs to understand yourself better.

- Embrace Vulnerability: Acknowledge your vulnerabilities and see them as opportunities for growth and self-improvement.

- Set Goals: Define clear, achievable goals that align with your values and aspirations.

- Build Resilience: Develop the ability to bounce back from setbacks and challenges with determination and strength.

- Cultivate Self-Awareness: Be mindful of your thoughts, emotions, and actions to enhance your self-understanding.

- Authenticity: Stay true to yourself and express your true thoughts and feelings without fear of judgment.

- Continuous Learning: Engage in lifelong learning to expand your knowledge, skills, and perspectives.

- Positive Mindset: Cultivate a positive attitude towards yourself, others, and life in general.

- Practice Empathy: Develop the ability to understand and connect with others on an emotional level.

- Take Action: Implement your plans, make decisions, and take proactive steps towards fulfilling your goals and aspirations.

By following these steps, you can begin to tap into your personal power, unlock your full potential, and embark on a journey towards greatness.

Chapter 2

Removing Self-Imposed Limitations

Self-imposed limitations are those invisible barriers we construct in our minds that prevent us from reaching our full potential. These limitations can manifest in different forms such as self-doubt, fear of failure, or negative self-talk. They restrict us from exploring new opportunities, pursuing our dreams, and living a fulfilling life. However, the key lies in recognizing and acknowledging these limitations to break free from their grasp.

Removing self-imposed limitations is a transformative journey that involves challenging your beliefs, stepping out of your comfort zone, and embracing change. It's about realizing that the power to shape your reality lies within you and that you have the ability to overcome any obstacle that stands in your way. By shedding these limitations, you open yourself up to a world of possibilities and unlock the immense potential that resides within you.

Each of us possesses a reservoir of untapped power waiting to be discovered. This power is not external but stems from within, fueled by our strengths, passions, and desires. When you know your strong points and nurture them, you cultivate a sense of purpose and confidence that propels you forward. Developing these strengths requires dedication, perseverance, and a willingness to push beyond your limits.

Taking time to reflect on your journey allows you to gain valuable insights into your motivations, goals, and areas for growth. It is through introspection that you uncover hidden talents, identify areas of improvement, and chart a course for personal development. Trusting what you feel inside about yourself is crucial in building self-assurance and self-belief. By listening to your intuition and honoring your inner voice, you align yourself with your true essence and tap into your innate power.

If you have yearned for that new home, car, or luxury vacation, know that you possess the potential to materialize these desires. The power to manifest your dreams lies in your hands, waiting to be harnessed through focused intention, strategic planning, and decisive action. By believing in your capabilities and taking proactive steps towards your goals, you can turn your aspirations into reality.

To embark on this journey of self-discovery and empowerment, it is essential to adopt a strategic approach. Identify your strengths, set clear goals, and formulate a plan of action that aligns with your vision. Trust that you have what it takes to overcome challenges, adapt to changes, and achieve success on your terms. Differentiate between what you should be doing to progress towards your goals and what you are actually doing in reality, confronting any discrepancies with honesty and determination.

Beware of falling into the traps of complacency and procrastination, as they can hinder your progress and perpetuate self-imposed limitations. Recognize the blockers in your path, whether they are external obstacles or internal doubts, and address them with resilience and resourcefulness. By staying vigilant and proactive, you can navigate through challenges, stay focused on your objectives, and unlock the boundless potential that lies within you; finding that place where you truly belong versus where you are.

Here are a few suggestions to start recognizing self-imposed limitations:

- Reflect on your beliefs: Take some time to reflect on your beliefs about yourself and your abilities. Are there any recurring thoughts or beliefs that make you feel limited or hold you back? Identifying these limiting beliefs is the first step in recognizing the limitations you have placed on yourself.

- Pay attention to self-talk: Listen to the way you talk to yourself. Are you constantly doubting your abilities or putting yourself down? Pay attention to any negative self-talk and recognize how it might be contributing to the limitations you have placed on yourself.

- Notice patterns in your behavior: Are there certain patterns in your behavior that indicate self-imposed limitations? For example, avoiding new opportunities or challenges because you believe you are not capable. Recognizing these patterns can help you understand the limitations you have set for yourself.

- Seek feedback from others: Sometimes, others can recognize our limitations more clearly than we can. Ask for feedback from trusted friends, family members, or mentors about any limitations they see in the way you approach your goals and aspirations.

- Consider past experiences: Reflect on past experiences where you may have held back or limited yourself due to fear or self-doubt. Understanding how these limitations have impacted your choices and actions can help you recognize similar patterns in the present.

By taking these steps, you can start to become more aware of the limitations they have placed on themselves. This self-awareness is a crucial first step in breaking free from these constraints and embracing their full potential.

Chapter 3

Overcoming Complacency and
Procrastination

Complacency and procrastination are two formidable foes that can sabotage our efforts to reach our full potential and hinder our path to greatness. They are insidious habits that lull us into a false sense of security and prevent us from taking the necessary steps towards our goals. Recognizing when you're intentionally putting something off or stagnating in a state of comfort is crucial to breaking free from these self-imposed limitations and unleashing the greatness within you.

Complacency is the silent killer of progress, disguised as contentment and comfort. It tricks us into settling for mediocrity, convincing us that we have reached a satisfactory level of achievement when, in reality, we are capable of so much more. Procrastination, on the other hand, is the thief of time and potential, robbing us of valuable opportunities and delaying our success through inaction.

To overcome complacency and procrastination, one must first acknowledge and confront these destructive behaviors head-on. It requires a conscious effort to push past the comfort zone, challenge the status quo, and embrace discomfort as a catalyst for growth. By recognizing the signs of complacency and procrastination in your life, you can take proactive measures to combat them and reclaim control over your actions and decisions.

Developing a sense of urgency and purpose is key to breaking free from complacency and procrastination. By setting clear goals, creating a sense of accountability, and establishing a structured plan of action, you can reignite your motivation and drive towards achieving your dreams. Cultivate a habit of prioritizing tasks, managing your time effectively, and consistently working towards your objectives, even when faced with obstacles or distractions.

It's essential to differentiate between productive rest and laziness, between strategic pauses and procrastination. While rest and relaxation are vital for maintaining a healthy balance in life, procrastination is a hinderance that stifles progress and diminishes your potential. Learn to listen to your inner voice and discern when you genuinely need a break versus when you are succumbing to procrastination out of fear or uncertainty.

By staying vigilant and self-aware, you can identify the triggers that lead to complacency and procrastination and develop strategies to overcome them. Create a supportive environment that fosters productivity, surround yourself with positive influences, and cultivate a mindset of growth and continuous improvement. Remember that the greatness and power within you deserve a chance to shine, and by pushing past self-imposed limitations, focusing on your goals, and taking decisive action, you can unlock your true potential and achieve incredible heights of success.

Recognizing when you're intentionally putting something off or stagnating in a state of comfort is crucial to breaking free from these self-imposed limitations and unleashing the greatness within you. Here are some suggestions to help overcome complacency and procrastination:

• Recognize the Signs: Acknowledge and understand the behaviors associated with complacency and procrastination. Awareness is the first step towards overcoming these habits.

- Set Clear Goals: Define specific, achievable goals that inspire and motivate you. Having a clear vision of what you want to accomplish can help combat complacency and procrastination.

- Establish Accountability: Create a system of accountability, whether it's by sharing your goals with a friend or using tools like goal-setting apps to track your progress.

- Create a Plan of Action: Break down your goals into actionable steps and create a structured plan to follow. This can provide direction and purpose, helping to overcome procrastination.

- Embrace Discomfort: Challenge the status quo and push past your comfort zone. Embracing discomfort as a catalyst for growth can help break the cycle of complacency.

- Prioritize Tasks: Develop the habit of prioritizing tasks and managing your time effectively. Setting priorities can help prevent procrastination and maintain focus.

- Differentiate Productive Rest from Procrastination: Learn to distinguish between strategic breaks for rest and relaxation and moments of procrastination driven by fear or uncertainty.

- Cultivate a Supportive Environment: Surround yourself with positive influences and create an environment that encourages productivity and personal growth.

- Stay Vigilant and Self-Aware: Pay attention to your thoughts and behaviors, and identify triggers that lead to complacency and procrastination.

- Take Decisive Action: Push past self-imposed limitations, stay focused on your goals, and consistently take decisive action towards achieving them.

By incorporating these steps into your daily life, you can begin to break free from complacency and procrastination, and work towards unleashing your full potential.

Chapter 4

Embracing Your Place of Power

True growth is about evolving, expanding, and stepping into your own power. It entails a profound self-discovery journey where you start to unravel the layers of who you truly are, as opposed to who you've always believed yourself to be.

The process of growth is not merely about age or experience; it goes much deeper. It demands a willingness to confront our fears, challenge our beliefs, and break free from limiting patterns and behaviors. As we navigate towards our locus of strength and authenticity, we begin to discern the stark contrast between our current selves and the person we are becoming.

Discovering our inherent power is a transformative experience. It involves recognizing and embracing our unique strengths, talents, and values. This awareness propels us towards shedding the old skins of insecurity, doubt, and conformity, and stepping boldly into our authentic selves.

However, with growth comes the inevitability of outgrowing the people, places, and situations that no longer align with our newfound essence. It's essential to understand that while you may have evolved and expanded, not everyone around you will share in that growth. It is a solo expedition that leads you to metamorphosis; expecting others to metamorphose alongside you can lead to disappointment and frustration.

I learned this lesson the hard way, to my detriment. In embracing change and personal growth, I was unthoughtful in assuming that those around me had grown. I was sorely mistaken. The pain and anguish I endured when a situation caused me to confront the reality that not everyone evolves at the same pace or in the same direction left me wounded and disillusioned.

It was a wake-up call—an invitation to recognize the one-sided nature of my expectations and assumptions. While I had transformed my perspectives, beliefs, and actions, those I held dear remained stagnant. My growth had inadvertently created a chasm between me and them, a gap that could not be bridged by wishful thinking or hopeful anticipation.

Growing into your place of power requires courage, conviction, and an unwavering sense of self-awareness. It beckons you to a seat at the table of authenticity, where your true essence is acknowledged, honored, and celebrated. Stepping into this realm demands that you leave behind the shadows of doubt, fear, and uncertainty, and embrace the radiant light of your genuine self.

As you walk into this transformative voyage, remember to discern where you belong and, equally important, where you no longer fit.

It is a journey of self-ownership and self-acceptance, a pilgrimage towards reclaiming your rightful place in the tapestry of existence.

Embrace your growth, honor your evolution, and cherish the blossoming of your authentic self. The path to your place of power is paved with self-discovery, resilience, and unwavering faith in your worth.

Here are a few suggestions to help embrace your place of power:

- Self-Reflection and Awareness: Start by reflecting on your beliefs, values, and behaviors. Identify areas where you may be holding yourself back or limiting your potential. Cultivate self-awareness to understand your strengths, weaknesses, and aspirations.

- Confront Fears and Challenge Beliefs: Courageously confront your fears and challenge beliefs that no longer serve you. Step out of your comfort zone and embrace uncertainty. Trust in your ability to overcome obstacles and embrace new opportunities for growth.

- Recognize Your Unique Strengths and Talents: Celebrate your unique strengths, talents, and values. Acknowledge the qualities that make you special and valuable. Embrace your individuality and use it as a source of empowerment in your personal and professional life.

- Let Go of Insecurity, Doubt, and Conformity: Release yourself from insecurity, doubt, and the pressure to conform. Embrace your authentic self with confidence and courage. Trust in your abilities and honor your worthiness to pursue your dreams and ambitions.

- Understand Evolving Relationships: Acknowledge that growth may lead to outgrowing certain relationships, environments, or situations. Be prepared to navigate these changes with grace and compassion. Understand that not everyone may evolve at the same pace or in the same direction as you.

- Practice Self-Compassion and Forgiveness: Be kind to yourself on your journey towards self-discovery and growth. Practice self-compassion and forgiveness for past mistakes or misjudgments. Allow yourself room for growth and learning from experiences, both positive and challenging.

- Embrace Your Authentic Self: Step boldly into your authenticity and embrace your true self. Release the burden of societal expectations and external pressures that hinder your self-expression. Celebrate the beauty of being your genuine self, honoring your uniqueness.

- Navigate Change with Resilience:As you evolve into your place of power, be resilient in the face of change and uncertainty. See challenges as opportunities for growth and learning. Trust in your inner strength and adaptability to navigate transitions with grace.

- Seek Support and Guidance: Surround yourself with supportive individuals who uplift and empower you on your journey. Seek guidance from mentors, coaches, or trusted friends who can offer insights and encouragement as you embrace your place of power.

- Practice Self-Care and Prioritize Your Well-being: Prioritize self-care and well-being as you embark on your journey of self-discovery and growth. Nurture your physical, emotional, and mental health to sustain your energy and resilience. Take time for activities that rejuvenate and inspire you along the way.

- Celebrate Your Progress and Achievements: Celebrate each milestone and achievement as you progress towards embracing your place of power. Acknowledge the growth and transformations you undergo, honoring the resilience and determination that guide you on this empowering journey.

Stay Committed to Your Evolution: Stay committed to your personal evolution and growth. Embrace the process of self-discovery as a continuous journey rather than a destination. Remain open to learning, adapting, and evolving as you step into your authentic power and reclaim your rightful place in the world.

Chapter 5

Positive Impact Upon Yourself

One of the most profound discoveries I made about myself was when I cleared away all the distractions, limitations, and external influences that were clouding my vision of who I truly am. It was in this space of clarity that I finally began to recognize my own superpowers. As I write this, I know that I have yet to reach my full potential, but I am certain that I am on the path to greatness. Why? Because I made a conscious effort to uncover and embrace the extraordinary power that resides within me, and to understand how best to harness it for the benefit of myself and others.

One of the remarkable aspects of my self-discovery journey is my innate ability to recognize greatness in others. Not only can I perceive the extraordinary potential within others, but what truly sets me apart is my capacity to draw out their latent power, shift their perspective with clarity, guide them in transforming their strengths into valuable assets, and offer multiple avenues for them to share their gifts with the world. Imagine someone who has been following a particular life trajectory for 30 years, feeling stuck and frustrated, yearning for a change but not knowing where to begin. I have this uncanny knack for identifying the unique abilities and untapped greatness in such individuals, and in some cases, I have helped them establish entire businesses based on their overlooked strengths.

It's a common phenomenon for people to be blind to their own capabilities and potential, which is why having the right support system and associations is crucial. Sometimes, we are the last to recognize our own brilliance, yet with the guidance of those who are attuned to their own strengths, some of us can swiftly pinpoint the abilities we possess. The truth is, it's imperative to swiftly align ourselves with our authentic selves, acknowledging our power and capabilities in order to fully maximize them for our own growth, to empower others, and to contribute to a better world. Yes, I proudly consider myself one of those individuals who are committed to creating a better world for all.

In essence, recognizing and embracing our innate gifts and talents is an essential step towards personal fulfillment and contributing meaningfully to the world around us. My journey has taught me that by tapping into our unique strengths, we not only fulfill our own potential but also become catalysts for positive change and transformation in the lives of others. This realization fills my heart with enthusiasm and purpose, propelling me forward in my mission to inspire and uplift those around me.

Remember, it's not just about discovering our individual strengths; it's about utilizing them to create a ripple effect of empowerment and positivity, ultimately shaping a world where everyone is encouraged to shine in their own unique way. So, as I continue on my path, I invite you to join me in acknowledging and celebrating the extraordinary power that resides within each of us, and let's embark on this journey of self-discovery and empowerment together. After all, a world where everyone recognizes and maximizes their potential is a world brimming with boundless opportunities for growth and prosperity.

Practical suggestions to a positive impact on both yourself and those around you:

- Clear Away Distractions: Begin by decluttering your physical and mental space. Create a peaceful environment that allows you to focus on self-reflection and introspection.

- Identify Your Superpowers: Take time to reflect on your strengths, passions, and talents. Consider what activities bring you joy and fulfillment, as these often hint at your unique abilities.

- Shift Perspective: Challenge any self-limiting beliefs or doubts that may be holding you back from recognizing your own greatness. Practice positive affirmations and gratitude to cultivate a growth mindset.

- Set Clear Goals: Define specific objectives that align with your strengths and aspirations. Break down these goals into actionable steps to move closer to realizing your full potential.

- Embrace Support Systems: Surround yourself with individuals who uplift and inspire you. Seek out groups where you can share your journey of self-discovery and receive encouragement along the way.

- Empower Others: Pay attention to the people around you and help them recognize their own strengths and potential. Offer guidance, support, and encouragement to those who may be struggling to see their own brilliance.

- Contribute to a Better World: Find ways to use your unique talents and abilities to make a positive impact in your community or beyond. Consider volunteering, mentoring, or starting a project that aligns with your values and strengths.

- Celebrate Growth: Acknowledge your progress and successes along the way. Celebrate both big milestones and small victories as you continue to unlock your extraordinary power and inspire others to do the same.

- Join the Journey: Embrace continuous self-discovery and empowerment. Stay open to new experiences, challenges, and opportunities that further expand your understanding of your capabilities and how you can contribute to a world filled with endless possibilities.

By following these practical steps and embracing your extraordinary power, you can embark on a transformative journey of self-discovery, empowerment, and positive impact on both yourself and those around you.

Chapter 6

How to Unveil Your Extraordinary Self

Make a conscious effort to acknowledge and embrace the extraordinary power that resides within you. This self-awareness not only benefits you but also equips you to positively influence those around you, creating a ripple effect of positivity and empowerment.

A crucial aspect of this journey is your ability to identify greatness in others. Look beyond surface qualities to perceive the untapped greatness within people. Cultivate the knack for extracting and honing their hidden talents, guiding them to leverage their strengths, and helping them showcase their unique gifts to the world. By lifting others up, you amplify the impact of your own journey. It's common to hinder our own potential by overlooking our capabilities. Surround yourself with a supportive community and mentors who can help you swiftly identify your latent talents. Aligning with your authentic self and acknowledging your power are foundational steps in maximizing personal growth, empowering others, and making a positive contribution to the world.

Embracing your innate gifts is more than personal fulfillment; it's a catalyst for positive change and transformation. By tapping into your unique strengths, you become a source of encouragement and inspiration for those around you. Recognize that your individual powers have the potential to create a ripple effect of empowerment and positivity in the world.

As you continue on your journey, extend an invitation to others to join you in celebrating the extraordinary power within themselves. Together, embark on a voyage of self-discovery and empowerment. A world where everyone realizes and maximizes their potential is a world brimming with endless possibilities for growth and prosperity. Remember, the key lies in unveiling your extraordinary self and embracing the journey towards empowerment and self-realization.

Here are practical steps to unveil your extraordinary self and embrace a journey towards empowerment and self-realization:

- Self-Awareness: Take time for self-reflection and acknowledge the extraordinary power within you. Recognize your unique strengths, talents, and capabilities. Understand that self-awareness not only benefits you but also equips you to positively influence those around you.

- Recognize Greatness in Others: Cultivate the ability to look beyond surface qualities and perceive the untapped potential within others. Encourage others to recognize and harness their latent talents by guiding them to leverage their strengths and showcase their unique gifts to the world.

- Build a Supportive Community: Surround yourself with a supportive community and mentors who can help you identify and maximize your latent talents. Seek guidance, mentorship, and collaboration to accelerate personal growth and empower others.

- Align with Authentic Self: Embrace your authentic self and acknowledge your innate gifts as foundational steps in maximizing personal growth and making a positive contribution to the world.

- Empower Others: By tapping into your unique strengths and embracing your innate gifts, become a source of encouragement and inspiration for those around you. Lift others up by sharing your knowledge, experiences, and support.

- Create a Ripple Effect: Recognize that your individual powers have the potential to create a ripple effect of empowerment and positivity in the world. Embracing your innate talents is more than personal fulfillment; it contributes to positive change and transformation on a broader scale.

- Celebrate Individual Potential: Encourage others to realize and maximize their potential. Create a supportive environment where everyone's unique strengths and capabilities are celebrated and leveraged for collective growth and prosperity.

By following these practical suggestions, you can unveil your extraordinary self, empower others, and contribute to a world where the true potential of every individual is recognized and celebrated.

Chapter 7

Breaking Through Blockers

For so long, I allowed my immediate environment and others' thoughts to cloud my judgement. I found myself held back and influenced by the expectations of others. The barriers I had imposed on myself seemed insurmountable, and the power within me felt distant and unattainable.

Recognizing and addressing these blockers was a necessary process. It took time, patience, and self-reflection to understand the impact they had on my life. I began to identify the patterns of thinking that were holding me back, and I made a conscious effort to confront them head-on. It wasn't easy, but with each small step, I felt a renewed sense of self, power, focus, strength and determination building within me.

Thinking I was unable to make it or complete my goal was another significant blocker that I needed to acknowledge. I realized that by letting go of these feelings, I could free myself from the paralyzing grip it held over me. I shifted my perspective to see incompletion as an opportunity for growth rather than a sign of incapability. This change in mindset gave me the courage to pursue my goals without falling short.

External influences played a role in shaping my limitations as well. Unknowingly, I had allowed the opinions and expectations of others to dictate my choices and actions, stifling my authenticity and potential. Taking ownership of my decisions and focusing on what truly mattered to me allowed me to break free from the constraints imposed by external pressures.

As I confronted these blockers, I began to feel a newfound sense of empowerment and liberation. The barriers that once seemed impenetrable started to crumble, revealing the power that had always existed within me. With each obstacle overcome, I gained confidence and momentum, propelling me toward the realization of my dreams and aspirations.

Trust became my guiding light through this journey. Trust in myself, my abilities, and the resilience that had always been present within me. It was through this unwavering trust that I found the courage to take action. I embraced the challenges that lay ahead, knowing that I possessed the strength and determination to overcome them.

Breaking through these blockers was not a solitary endeavor. It required support, encouragement, and a belief in the potential that resided within me. As I removed the self-imposed limitations, I discovered a reservoir of untapped power waiting to be unleashed. I watched in awe as my potential unfolded before me, revealing a future filled with possibility and promise.

The journey to breaking through blockers was arduous, but the rewards were immeasurable. As I stand on the other side, I can attest to the transformative power of confronting and overcoming these barriers. Trust in yourself, take action, and witness the remarkable extent of your power unfold before you. Embrace the freedom that comes with shedding self-imposed limitations and step into the boundless potential that awaits on the other side.

Practical suggestions for breaking through blockers:

- Identify Limiting Beliefs: Begin by recognizing the negative thoughts and patterns that are holding you back. Be honest with yourself about the fears and doubts that have influenced your decisions and actions.

- Practice Self-Reflection: Set aside regular time for introspection and self-discovery. Journaling or meditative practices can help you delve into the root causes of your blockers and gain clarity on how they have impacted your life.

- Confront Negative Patterns: Take proactive steps to confront and challenge the negative patterns of thinking that have limited your potential. Replace self-limiting beliefs with affirmations and positive mindset exercises.

- Reclaim Ownership: Evaluate the influence of external pressures and expectations on your decision-making. Focus on reclaiming ownership of your choices, values, and aspirations, and resist the constraints imposed by external influences.

- Cultivate Trust: Build trust in yourself and your abilities. Reflect on past accomplishments and strengths, reinforcing the confidence in your capacity to overcome obstacles and achieve your aspirations.

- Seek Support: Surround yourself with a supportive network of friends, or mentors, or professionals who can provide encouragement and guidance as you navigate through breaking through your blockers.

- Take Action: Start with small, manageable steps to push past your blockers. Each incremental success will build momentum and reinforce your belief in your ability to overcome challenges.

- Celebrate Progress: Acknowledge and celebrate each milestone as you break through your blockers. Recognize the strength and resilience you demonstrate with each obstacle overcome.

- Embrace Empowerment: As you witness the dissolution of your self-imposed limitations, allow yourself to embrace the freedom and empowerment that comes with shedding these barriers. Step into your renewed sense of potential and embrace the boundless opportunities that await.

By following these practical steps and committing to confront and overcome your blockers, you can embark on a transformative journey towards unlocking your true potential and experiencing the immeasurable rewards that accompany this process.

Chapter 8

Your Power Is In Your Purpose

Your power is in your purpose. Whatever it is you're supposed to be doing in the world, there lies your power. The key is to get to the point and figure that out as quickly as possible. The answer to that is taking a look inside of you and understanding the thing you enjoy doing, that thing that makes you feel free and liberated, that brings you joy, and even though you're earning revenue, it does not feel like work. It's thrilling and makes you feel alive, energized, and excited.

When you begin to feel a twinge of these emotions, that is the direction you want to pursue and test to see if that is it. Generally, at least what I found for myself is when I looked back at my years as a teen, I can see that one thing that was always there, but it never developed because either my parents or situations shaped my life differently. Fortunately, for me, the core of me was never allowed to be buried; it continued to peak out like a green plant budding above concrete, and we simply can't figure out how. That is until we see the crack that gave it a small break to burst through.

Well, that's me and that's still you. My hope is this book is a gateway to your power, which is interlaced with your purpose. Take the time to ponder over what you enjoy doing as a person, as an individual. Of course, that is only the surface because there are things about you that you are en route to discovering. We are complex, unique, and mighty beings filled with immense genius and greatness in our own way.

So, continue to take the time to explore and uncover your purpose. Your power lies within it, waiting to be unleashed. Once you tap into that, there's no limit to what you can achieve. You'll find the drive, the passion, and the determination to pursue your purpose with everything you've got. And that, my friend, is where true power lies. It's in living a life that's aligned with your purpose, where every action you take is fueled by your passion and your drive to make a difference in the world. So, don't underestimate the power of your purpose. It's the key to unlocking your true potential and living a life that's truly fulfilling. Embrace it, nurture it, and let it guide you to greatness. Your power is in your purpose.

Delving deeper into your individuality and uncovering unique qualities and strengths is a deeply personal and introspective journey. Here are some suggestions for you to explore individuality:

- Identify passions and interests: Make a list of the things that genuinely excite and inspire you. Consider hobbies, activities, or subjects that you find yourself drawn to, even if they seem unrelated to your current work or daily life.

- Embrace curiosity: Be open to new experiences and opportunities. Engage in activities that pique your curiosity and challenge you to step outside your comfort zone. This can help you discover hidden talents and interests.

- Connect with mentors: Seek out mentors or role models who can offer guidance and support as you explore your individuality and potential. Their wisdom and experiences can provide valuable perspectives.

- Experiment and learn: Take on new challenges, pursue learning opportunities, and experiment with different activities. This can help you uncover talents and strengths that you may not have realized you possessed.

- Embrace authenticity: Be true to yourself

and embrace your uniqueness. Avoid comparing yourself to others and focus on developing your own strengths and qualities. Authenticity is key to unlocking your potential.

- Engage in New Experiences: Embrace curiosity and open-mindedness by seeking out new experiences and challenges. Whether it's learning a new skill or exploring a new hobby, these experiences can help you uncover hidden talents and interests.

- Embrace Your Purpose: Once you've uncovered your purpose, embrace it wholeheartedly. Allow it to guide your decisions and actions, and let it fuel your passion and determination to make a positive impact in the world.

- Take Action: Armed with a clear sense of purpose, take proactive steps to align your life with your newfound clarity. Embrace your purpose, nurture it, and let it guide you toward a life filled with fulfillment and greatness.

By following these suggestions, you can embark on a journey of self-discovery, uncover your purpose, and unleash the power that comes from living a life aligned with your true passions and aspirations.

Chapter 9

Don't Underestimate Yourself

It's easy to underestimate your abilities, especially when faced with new challenges or opportunities. But the truth is, you have more potential within you than you may realize. When given the chance, your talent, creativity, and true power will shine through, leaving those around you in awe.

Whether you're an entrepreneur, seeking a new career opportunity, or stepping into the next level of your personal or professional life, it's important to recognize your true worth. Take the time to do your homework and understand the market value for your unique talents. Don't just rely on what comes to mind or what you think you should be worth. Your true value may surprise you.

Undervaluing oneself can have significant impacts on both personal and professional growth. When one underestimates their worth and abilities, they may inadvertently hinder their own progress and potential success.

In a professional context, undervaluing oneself can lead to missed opportunities for career advancement. It may result in accepting lower compensation than what one truly deserves, which can have long-term financial implications. Additionally, it can lead to being overlooked for promotions or important projects, as others may not recognize the full extent of your capabilities.

On a personal level, undervaluing oneself can impact confidence and self-esteem. This can manifest in various aspects of life, including relationships, decision-making, and overall well-being. It may also lead to a lack of assertiveness and difficulty in setting boundaries, which can affect personal and professional relationships.

Furthermore, undervaluing oneself can limit the willingness to take risks and pursue new challenges. This can stifle personal growth and prevent people from reaching their full potential. It can also create a cycle of self-doubt, as one may continue to underestimate their abilities, leading to a lack of motivation and initiative.

Overall, undervaluing oneself can create barriers to personal and professional growth, affecting both opportunities and overall fulfillment. Recognizing and acknowledging your worth and capabilities is crucial for fostering growth, confidence, and success in all aspects of life.

When you align your work with your natural gifts and abilities, you may find that you've underestimated yourself. This realization can also mean that you've been underpricing your skills and contributions. It's crucial to recognize the value you bring to the table and to convey that to others.

So, don't sell yourself short. Embrace your talents, creativity, and power. When you start and complete your work with confidence and passion, you'll realize that you are capable of much more than you ever imagined. By recognizing and harnessing your true potential, you can set yourself up for success and fulfillment in all aspects of your life. Don't underestimate yourself; you are capable of achieving great things.

Overcoming the habit of undervaluing yourself is essential for personal growth and career success. Here are some suggestions to address this:

- Self-Reflection: Take time to reflect on your strengths, accomplishments, and the value you bring to your work. Recognize your skills and contributions, and understand the impact you have on your team and organization.

- Set Clear Goals: Establish clear professional goals and objectives for yourself. Having a clear sense of what you want to achieve can help you focus on your strengths and the value you bring to your work.

- Develop Assertiveness: Practice assertiveness by communicating your ideas, needs, and accomplishments confidently. This can include speaking up in meetings, negotiating for fair compensation, and advocating for opportunities that align with your skills and interests.

- Update Your Skills: Continuously invest in your professional development by acquiring new skills and knowledge. This can boost your confidence and demonstrate your commitment to growth and excellence in your field.

- Network and Build Relationships: Engage with networks and build positive relationships. Networking can provide opportunities to share your expertise, gain recognition, and expand your professional support system.

- Practice Self-Advocacy: Take an active role in advocating for yourself in professional settings. This can involve participating in performance reviews, discussing career advancement opportunities, and negotiating for fair compensation.

- Embrace Growth Mindset: Cultivate a growth mindset, viewing challenges as opportunities for learning and development. Embracing a mindset focused on growth and resilience can help you overcome self-doubt and undervaluation.

- Visualize Success: Visualization techniques involve imagining yourself achieving your goals and overcoming challenges. This can help build confidence and create a positive mindset that supports your efforts.

By taking these steps, you can work towards overcoming the habit of undervaluing themselves, leading to increased confidence, recognition, and career advancement.

Chapter 10

Getting on Track

When I first ventured into the world of entrepreneurship, I eagerly leaped into action, relying on my existing knowledge and resources. While some of those early approaches are still valuable, the way I navigate the entrepreneurial landscape now is a stark contrast to my previous method. Unbridled passion, I discovered, can sometimes hinder progress and obscure your true greatness. There came a point where my relentless work ethic and impassioned approach began to work against me, leading to a sense of frustration and disillusionment.

The watershed moment arrived when I recognized that this was not how my life was meant to unfold. I knew, deep within, that my talents and worth should yield greater financial rewards and have a far-reaching impact, all while leaving me with a profound sense of fulfillment and happiness. Realizing that this was not materializing, I understood that I needed to chart a new course for myself.

I had played a part in veering off track, and I bore the responsibility of redirecting my trajectory. It required shedding the influences and relationships that had led me astray and had toiled to save myself from the unsatisfactory place I found myself in. I vividly recall standing in my kitchen in the dead of night, tears silently streaming down my face as I grappled with the overwhelming sense of discontent. This moment marked the commencement of my journey back to where I knew I belonged, away from the self-imposed hole I had dug.

With strategic intention and unwavering determination, I set out to extricate myself from that self-imposed pit. If you ever find yourself in a similar situation, understand that it is never too late to reclaim your winning hand. It demands concerted effort – both internal and external – to pave the way forward, but I stand as living proof that you possess the capacity to realign yourself toward your desired path.

Reflecting on that defining period in my life, I am struck by the wealth of invaluable lessons I gleaned, particularly in discerning what resonates with my true self and what does not. Those experiences equipped me with the insight and resilience needed to play my winning hand and reap the rewards it brings. You, too, hold a winning hand within you; the crucial task lies in uncovering it.

I firmly believe that life presents an abundance of winning hands, each harboring the potential to materialize the dreams we hold. Yet, many fail to invest the necessary time to nurture their strengths, recalibrate their mindset, manage their time effectively, or heed the gentle nudges emanating from their inner being, even when unfamiliar. Breaking free from the confines of familiarity is pivotal in paving the way toward the realization of our dreams. We all harbor aspirations, and if we can conceive them, it is likely that they are well within our grasp, waiting to be unlocked from within.

Regardless of your origins or past circumstances, as human beings, we possess the innate capacity to ascend to our full potential, given the opportunity. Every individual is inherently poised for success, and it is imperative that we afford ourselves the chance to actualize it.

Here are a few suggestions on how to realign, and get back on track:

- Self-Reflection and Accountability: Take a moment to reflect on your current situation and acknowledge the factors that have led you off track. Accept responsibility for your circumstances and understand that change begins with self-awareness.

- Identify Limiting Influences: Evaluate the people, habits, and beliefs that may be hindering your progress. It's crucial to distance yourself from negative influences and surround yourself with those who support your growth and development.

- Embrace Strategic Intention and Determination: Set clear goals for yourself and commit to pursuing them with unwavering determination. Develop a strategic plan that outlines the steps needed to reclaim your path and achieve your desired outcomes.

- Cultivate Resilience and Insight: Draw upon the lessons learned from past experiences to cultivate resilience and insight. Use these insights to navigate challenges and make informed decisions that align with your true self.

- Uncover Your Winning Hand: Recognize that you possess a unique set of strengths and capabilities that can lead to success and fulfillment. Invest time in nurturing these strengths, recalibrating your mindset, and managing your time effectively to unleash your full potential.

- Listen to Your Inner Being: Pay attention to your intuition and inner nudges, even when they feel unfamiliar. Breaking free from the confines of familiarity is essential for unlocking your true aspirations and realizing your dreams.

- Afford Yourself the Opportunity for Success: Regardless of your background or past circumstances, understand that you have the innate capacity to achieve success. Grant yourself the chance to actualize your potential and embrace the opportunities that lie ahead.

By following these suggestions, you can initiate the process of realigning your journey and finding fulfillment. Remember that you hold the power to reclaim your path and pave the way toward the realization of your dreams. The key lies in self-reflection, determination, and embracing your innate strengths to achieve success and happiness.

Chapter 11

I Know Who I Am

When you reach that pivotal moment where you can confidently declare, "I know who I am," it becomes paramount to cling onto that sense of self with unwavering strength. Refuse to let external forces cloud your perception or convince you to downplay the extraordinary aspects you've uncovered within yourself.

After gaining a solid understanding of your identity and strengths, it's crucial to embrace your authenticity and stand firm in your beliefs. Recognize your inherent value and uniqueness, understanding that you are a rare gem, irreplaceable in your entirety. The world anticipates the full expression of the exceptional qualities that set you apart.

Bestow the world with the gift of your presence, radiating as the magnificent gem that you are. Embrace your individuality and allow your inner light to illuminate your path forward. By honoring and treasuring the depths of your being, you not only empower yourself but also serve as a source of inspiration for those around you, encouraging them to embrace their own distinctiveness with confidence and grace.

Fully embracing and celebrating all facets of your being is not just a gift to yourself but a gift to the world. Hold tight to your power, cherish your unique attributes, and step into the world with unwavering certainty, showcasing the brilliance of the extraordinary gem that you are. Your authenticity serves as a radiant beacon that has the power to shine light on the world in ways that are truly transformative and awe-inspiring.

Maintaining a strong sense of self-worth and personal power in the face of external influences can be challenging, but it is essential for personal growth and well-being.

Here are some strategies to help maintain a sense of self-worth and power:

- Self-Awareness: The first step is to know who you are. Take the time to understand your values, strengths, and weaknesses. Self-awareness allows you to have a clear understanding of your worth and the power you possess as an individual.

- Set Boundaries: Establishing healthy boundaries is crucial for protecting your sense of self-worth. Learn to say no to things that do not align with your values or make you feel uncomfortable. Setting boundaries shows that you value yourself and your well-being.

- Surround Yourself with Supportive People: Seek out relationships and friendships with individuals who uplift and support you. Surrounding yourself with positive influences can help reinforce your sense of self-worth and power.

- Practice Self-Compassion: Be kind to yourself and practice self-compassion. Treat yourself with the same kindness and understanding that you would offer to a friend. Self-compassion can help you maintain a positive self-image and inner strength.

- Seek Growth Opportunities: Engage in activities that promote personal growth and development. Pursuing new skills and experiences can boost your confidence and reinforce your sense of personal power.

- Seek Professional Help if Needed: If external influences are significantly impacting your self-worth and power, consider seeking support from a therapist or counselor. Professional help can provide valuable tools and strategies to strengthen your sense of self-worth.

By practicing self-awareness, setting boundaries, surrounding yourself with supportive people, practicing self-compassion, challenging negative thoughts, seeking growth opportunities, and seeking professional help if needed, you can maintain their sense of self-worth and power in the face of external influences. Remember, you are capable, valuable, and deserving of respect and self-worth.

Chapter 12

Guarding Your Power: Navigating External Influences with Confidence and Clarity

In a world filled with diverse opinions, personal experiences, and influential figures, it can be a challenge to retain your sense of self-worth and power in the face of external pressures. It's crucial to value and safeguard your identity and all the wonderful attributes you have discovered about yourself along your journey.

Protecting your power does not mean isolating yourself from others, although there are instances where maintaining a safe distance is necessary. Being discerning about the company you keep is essential – not everyone deserves to access the essence of your being. While new acquaintances may flock to you, it's important to consider the impact they may have on your personal resources and well-being before forming close bonds.

When confronted with unsolicited advice or suggestions on how to navigate your path, it's imperative not to let irritation cloud your judgment. Remember, some people genuinely believe they are offering their best guidance, even if it may not align with your needs or aspirations. Learn to safeguard your ears from words that do not serve you, allowing them to slide off without affecting the core of who you are. If advice doesn't resonate with your truth, gracefully move on, maintaining a shield of confidence around your newfound self.

By recognizing the importance of selectively absorbing external influences and staying true to your authentic self, you can confidently navigate through the sea of opinions and experiences, emerging stronger and more empowered in your own unique essence.

Here are some suggestions to help protect you identity and inner strength amidst external pressures:

- Value Your Identity: Take time to acknowledge and appreciate all the wonderful qualities and discoveries about yourself that make you unique. Recognize that your identity is precious and should be safeguarded against influences that may seek to diminish it.

- Be Selective in Your Connections: Understand that not everyone you meet is meant to have access to the essence of who you are. Exercise discernment in choosing the company you keep, considering how their presence may impact your personal well-being and resources.

- Handle Unsolicited Advice Wisely: When faced with advice or suggestions that don't resonate with your truth, avoid letting irritation cloud your judgment. Remember that some people may genuinely believe they are helping you, even if their guidance doesn't align with your needs or goals.

- Safeguard Your Ears: Learn to filter out words and opinions that do not serve your growth or contribute positively to your journey. Allow irrelevant advice to slide off without affecting your core beliefs or sense of self.

- Stay True to Yourself: Embrace your authentic self and trust in your own intuition and wisdom. Maintain a shield of confidence around your newfound self, ensuring that external influences do not sway you from your path.

By implementing these suggestions and recognizing the importance of protecting your power, you can confidently navigate through the myriad of external influences, emerging stronger and more empowered in your own unique essence.

Chapter 13

Thriving in the Journey - Living a Life of
Purpose and Satisfaction

Each of us is a unique thread woven with care and purpose. As you journey through the realms of self-discovery, embracing your talents, abilities, and the sheer essence of who you are, remember to flourish in every step forward. It is not mere existence but living vibrantly that transforms the ordinary into extraordinary.

Let your newfound understanding of yourself be the beacon guiding you towards a life of purpose and satisfaction. Embrace the journey with open arms, for within this path lies a plethora of opportunities waiting to be seized. Revel in the joy of discovering your true self, and let each realization fuel your ascent towards becoming the best version of yourself.

As you navigate the twists and turns of life,

remember to thrive, not just survive. Happiness, joy, and fulfillment are not destinations but companions on this exhilarating ride. Let your purpose permeate every fiber of your being, allowing its radiance to illuminate your path. In doing so, you will exude a sunshine so bright that it touches the hearts of those around you.

In basking in your purpose, you will find not only satisfaction but a deep sense of contentment that transcends the mundane. Cherish each moment, relish each triumph, and learn from each setback, for it is in these experiences that your true essence shines through. Embrace life in its fullness, revel in the beauty of your journey, and let the power within you guide you towards a life filled with meaning and significance.

Epilogue

As you reach the final pages of "The Power Within," take a moment to reflect on the incredible journey you've embarked upon. Through the transformative chapters of this book, you've delved deep into the essence of your being, uncovering layers of potential and strength that have long been dormant within you.

You've learned that true greatness is not found in external achievements or accolades, but in the quiet confidence and unwavering power that resides at your core. It is the ability to tap into this wellspring of inner strength, to embrace your authenticity, and to stand in your truth, that sets you on the path to extraordinary impact and fulfillment.

As you continue to chip away at the self-imposed limitations and societal expectations that may have clouded your vision, remember that the journey of self-discovery is not always easy. There will be moments of pondering, moments of isolation, and moments where the weight of expectation feels heavy upon your shoulders. But through it all, hold fast to the knowledge that within you lies a reservoir of untapped potential waiting to be unleashed.

The true essence of your power lies not in how others perceive you, but in how you perceive yourself. It is in the unwavering commitment to fully embracing your true self, flaws and strengths alike, that you will find the liberation and empowerment you seek.

So, as you close this chapter of your journey and step out into the world anew, remember this - you are a force of nature, a beacon of light, and a vessel of limitless potential. Embrace this truth, nurture it, and let it guide you as you navigate the complexities of life with grace and purpose.

The power within you is a gift waiting to be unwrapped, a treasure waiting to be discovered. Embrace it, own it, and let its brilliance shine forth for all the world to see. For in your true power lies the capacity to shape not only your own destiny but also the destiny of those around you.

Step boldly into your greatness, and may the journey ahead be filled with endless possibilities, boundless joy, and the unshakeable knowledge that the power within you is truly limitless.

www.ingramcontent.com/pod-product-compliance
Lightning Source LLC
Chambersburg PA
CBHW021003150626
46549CB00012BA/1041